COOKOUT

FOREWORD

Cookout is a part of Lucky Jefferson's collaborative arc of issues.

This arc prioritizes escapism while offering new ways for writers to challenge themselves and their present writing styles. I knew I wanted to publish a "dinner party" type of issue and with summer on the precipice and the flowers slowly creeping from places unseen, I felt a 'cookout' would be a perfect addition to our library.

One thing I looked forward to seeing the most is how writers would work with, challenge, bend the parameters of this given issue; in this case, it was how each writer creatively "showed up" for our cookout. I loved witnessing how writers reinvigorated the every day poem or flash fiction in the context of a cookout or dinner party.

This issue brings so many joys I experienced as a child out of slumber. From cakewalks, to BBQs, to your end-of-year cookout, I am grateful that authors created a reality that hasn't existed for many of us in a long time. I am thankful that each of the writers included in this issue dared to step beyond reality and dream; past the bleakness or trauma many of us have come to know.

This issue is representative of the many ways we can continue preserving our community—a reminder that we will, one day, be able to come together again.

NABEELA WASHINGTON
EDITOR IN CHIEF

Copyright © 2021 *Lucky Jefferson*.

All rights reserved. This book or any portion thereof may not be reproduced or used in any manner whatsoever without the express written permission of the publisher except for the use of brief quotations in a book review.

Printed in the United States of America.

ISBN 978-1-956076-99-8

ISSUE DESIGN and PROOFREADING by NaBeela Washington
COVER ART by Shashi Arnold and Liliana Melgar

Shashi Arnold is an aspiring illustrator and was the art editor of Montgomery Blair High School's newspaper *Silver Chips*. Shashi plans to study illustration at Pratt Institute.

Liliana Melgar graduated from Montgomery College with a degree in Illustration, aspires to work in animation, and loves using interesting color schemes and movement in her illustrations.

Publication of *Lucky Jefferson* is made possible through community support.

Donate or submit to *Lucky Jefferson* on our website: luckyjefferson.com.

COOKOUT MENU & FESTIVITIES

LINDA MCMULLEN	COLESLAW
ANNETTE GAGLIARDI	ONION RYE BUNS
CRISTINA LEGARDA	AIOLI
ANTHONY CORDASCO	TOMATO HORNWORM
CAMILLE FERGUSON	JALAPENO POPPERS
C. T. HOLTE	SHARP
ERIN MCDONOUGH	COUSINS
ROBERT BEVERIDGE	MILK TEETH
MIAH PRESCOD	BACKYARD JAM
LAUREN EVANS	FISH FRY
MAYA LEWIS	EVERYBODY HERE
JARED PEARCE	DODGEBALL
ANDRE PELTIER	MEXICAN SLAYRIDE: MARK 2
MIRANDA RODRIGUEZ	SOON

BACKYARD JAM

      I heard
we gon be outside this summer
and what better way to welcome
the blossoming of her presence
than a cookout --
an ode to the breeze and warmth
from her sun goddess gaze.
Let's call it a tribute.
One phone call and
everybody coming home to
aunty's hands in the kitchen working her magic.
But is it really a cookout if you don't ask
who made the mac and cheese?
Cause everybody's hands ain't like aunty's hands.
      Or my mother's.
The grill is calling my uncle's name
searching for chicken
hot dogs lined up waiting.
I like mine burnt.
That's the only way to do it.
Mango chow straight from the islands.
If you can't handle peppa this ain't for you.

This is a backyard jam and
we bringing Trinidad across the sea
straight into Brooklyn.

MIAH PRESCOD

JALAPENO POPPERS

Dad's been in the kitchen before the sun
made it to the party, & I woke to the sweet
smell of herbed cream cheese folded
in sausage, laid in a jalapeno bed.
For a man with fingers like sausages,
he's nimble in there, tender
in the soft glow of oven light.
I see my face reflected
when he watches guests ingest—
it's almost impolite, bad manners, how much we care.
Food is our love language, & we've never loved quite
right. I'm never around for this anymore,
the quiet hours of preparation. I show up
to the party & I've missed it.

CAMILLE FERGUSON

TOMATO HORNWORM

I will hear you
Eating
if I am patient.
But I see your destruction,
the skeletal remains
of vital leaves,
and impetuously
begin again
to touch
gently,
all those
vibrant green as you
remaining;
turn them over
searching for your fat round body,
bright yellow tiger stripes.
voracious
and ravenous
Eater
to be heard and hunted.

You remain elusive
and I am reduced
to scatology.

I have been witness
to your
Hawk Moth
transformation,
(colors brown and gold to pink and grey),
but I am
too impatient for a promise
of what may be
and concerned,
more,
for what I can feast on
now.

ANTHONY CORDASCO

FISH FRY

It is a Fish Fry in Anse La Raye
and the music hums through the valley
like the droning of the click-clacks
in the morning. The beat slides
sinuously up the hills, like a fer-de-lance
gliding through the long grasses,
eyes on its next meal. From my spot
in the bathroom, the song calls to me
and the lights of the town are a beacon
against the blackness of the night
and the thousand shots of starlight
that hang above like permanently stationed
fireflies. The main street,
the only real street, is likely more packed
than it is during the day, only
with bodies and the beat and the scent
of frying food, instead of choking
car smoke and the hawking calls of vendors
longing to sell their wares.
The music tickles the banana bags
in the trees as it swarms towards our house
on the bluff. My mind urges me towards
dancing, but they don't teach you how a mambo
in cotillion. But all I can hear is spices
carried on a cool night breeze and sliding bone-
white piano keys are pushed far out of my mind in
favor of the drums that carry the beat. I open the
window wider, lean out farther, and let the air play
on my face, imagining myself
down on the street of the town, spinning
into a harmony-drunk fever.

LAUREN EVANS

LUCKY JEFFERSON'S LITERARY ARTISTS

Johnny Yat Kiu Chan + Ivonne Manon designed the artwork on pages 12-13.

Ivonne Manon is a Dominican Illustrator based In Florida. She loves illustrating dynamic, dream-like scenes with a bunch of wiggly shapes. When she's not drawing she loves spending her days imagining fantasy adventures.

Yat (Johnny) is an illustrator inspired by nature and reality, he is passionate in making the audience have a great time reading his illustrations while bringing a message across. Also, he is quirky.

COOKOUT BINGO

GOT BINGO? EMAIL YOUR RESULTS TO
SUBMISSIONS@LUCKYJEFFERSON.COM FOR A PRIZE.

Enter **BINGO** into the ***Subject Line*** of your email.

Try a food mentioned in *Cookout*	Show another writer in *Cookout* some love	Write a poem using a line from a piece published in *Cookout*
Snap a photo with your copy of *Cookout* & tag us	Write in a new environment *(the weirder the better)*	Send a new piece to a mag that has declined your work
Write a poem about the tastiest thing you've eaten in the last 24 hours	Try cooking a new recipe	Read a poem you wrote that you dislike to a friend or family member
Pay it forward. Donate food you don't need to a local food shelter	Attend a local open mic	Write about the first food you see during your next trip to the grocery store

Aioli requires near-perfect silence.
It won't withstand the roil
of household noise – footfall,
crockery, speech, slamming doors.
Speak in whispers if you must,
lest the crushed garlic, egg
yolks, salt, and olive oil
fail to mingle drop by drop.

A kiss of lemon juice, perhaps,
to bring the brightness of the sun
into the toil of pestle grinding garlic
on the stone – but lightly, a troubadour's
caress on strings, like the heady scent
of lavender and loam, or the faint tolling
of an old church bell just faraway enough
to leave the mingling undisturbed.

Another drop – but not quite there;
the labor slow as slants of light,
their languid length across the kitchen wall
a stretching of space and time, the world.

This is the drop, this is the one:
shhhhh
we've already come so far.
A whisking full of hope, a pause.

The drop has disappeared from sight.
A new creation now is here
to soak into our eager bread,
to melt over our tongues
like a dollop of poetry,
luxurious and nourishing,
with just enough bite.

CRISTINA LEGARDA

ONION RYE BUNS

When the fat is rendered to a fine, clear ghee
and the pan is coated with it, tenderly;
when the yeast has done it's magic to the flour,
and the dough has risen to its finest hour;
when onion bits jump like crickets in heat
while you stretch and pull the doughy meat
into the round mounds of satisfaction,
then place on that pan's ready attraction;

when the towel is placed oh, so carefully
over buns now sitting, successfully
under stove lights that will do the rest
to make this savory dish the best,
and urge from the lips of the repast takers
requests of *"More, please!"* for these bun-bakers.

ANNETTE GAGLIARDI

MILK TEETH

Curdsqueak liminal against the tongue,
muted by the thick brown of a gravy
simmered low since dawn. Conversation
about alien abduction, the edge
of the world, nanotechology hidden
in your doctor's syringes cannot dull
the subtle resistance, perfect snap
of the fry, sharp heat against the tongue
less a price to be paid than a gatekeeper
against those who would trade it off
for room-temperature sog. But above
it all, the brown beef steam, the wonder
at how many organisms in this magic
concoction have been modified.

ROBERT BEVERIDGE

SHARP

When I was about eleven, I got
my first hunting knife.
As I had nothing to hunt,
it mostly sliced tomatoes at picnics.

Then at fifteen, a relative in Norway
gifted me a Mora knife from Sweden,
great for whittling. Dad appropriated it
to slice and butter the hamburger buns.

My brother-in-law gave me
a fine "Pony" pocketknife for Christmas.
I kept this little darling in my pocket,
sharpened sticks for marshmallow roasts.

The kitchen knife drawer now overflows
with top-end tools from Germany
for every kind of slicing and dicing,
but they are too good to take outside.

Last trip, the best kitchen store in Minneapolis
sold me a lovely chef's knife for only $29.95.
Finally! Into the picnic basket it went.
Now if it would ever stop raining . . .

C. T. HOLTE

COLESLAW

My best friend Jen texted, *We should definitely get everyone together one last time! How's August 12?* – and my heart constricted.

I texted back, *Sounds great!*

She responded, *Dad says we can use the backyard for a cookout.*

Then added, *I'm thinking hot dogs, hamburgers.*

Next, *Do you think we should go old school and do S'Mores too?*

And, *Hey, is everything OK?*

I wrote, *We should get black bean burgers for Sara and Kelsey.*

She replied, *<3*

Mom, tight-lipped, said, "Well, Kaitlyn, are you ready?"

"Let's go," I said. I grabbed a cardigan; Dr. Jansen's office was consistently over-air conditioned and the wait times in the pink paper gowns skewed long.

In the run-up to the party, I helped Jen confirm attendance (Sara, Kelsey, Derek, Tom, Naomi, Makayla, Terrence, and Quinn said they could come; the Ryland twins were off camping), purchase cheesy decorations at the dollar store, and discuss the menu. "I'm thinking we want to go uber-traditional," she said. "Sodas, chips, a fruit salad, corn on the cob, a green salad, coleslaw…"

The very idea of mayonnaise turned my stomach. "Um… sounds good."

"Cupcakes or s'mores?"

"Cupcakes," I said. Those always went down easily.

Jen said, "Awesome. Oh, I meant to tell you, I got an email from my future roommate today!"

One more thing I wouldn't… "Wow," I said. "Does she seem nice?"

"A little churchy, but fine." Jen peered at me. "I mean, she can't replace *you*."

I smiled. "Ah, I wasn't worried about *that*."

"So remind me about your major?" asked Jen's mom, as I put the finishing touches on the beverage table. I fidgeted with the ice bucket – then an almighty crash sounded within the house. "Jason!" screamed Jen's mom. "Your sister's having a party, do you have to –"

The doorbell rang, and I said, "I'll get it, Mrs. Lewandowski."

It was Derek. He grunted, "You OK?"

I shrugged.

Makayla turned up then, with ice cream, so I helped her Tetris-repack the Lewandowskis' overstuffed freezer. The others arrived. Jen's dad manned the grill and only offered a couple of derogatory remarks ending in *veggie burgers*.

Quinn had put together a nostalgia-tinged playlist, starting with Sarah McLachlan's "I Will Remember You"; Kelsey and Terrence were dancing and pretending they weren't in earnest. Talk turned to college – majors, clubs, whether or not to go Greek. I nodded along.

Then Jen's mom came out to check on us. I was deciding between a slice of watermelon and some grapes when she said, "Oh, Kaitlyn, honey, you've hardly got anything! Let me help you out!" and she piled coleslaw onto my plate.

Vomit rose in my throat; I turned to sprint toward the bathroom. I didn't make it more than four feet through the Lewandowskis' yard.

Shock, horror, then the inevitable fluttering: paper towels / cup of water / have a seat. Derek volunteered to sit with me in the Lewandowskis' cool living room while Jen went to find a new shirt for me to borrow. "So that's still happening," he said.

"It doesn't necessarily stop the minute the first trimester ends," I muttered.

Jen brought down a slithery tank top I'd long admired. I bit my lip. "I'm so sorry," I said. "I don't think it's going to fit anymore."

She looked from the top, to me, to the grim-faced Derek kneeling beside me, and paled. "Kaitlyn…"

"Yes," I said, brusquely. "Four months in. Due in January. Not going to school."

"Not *now*," Derek interjected. "I'll go first, and then…"

And then. The future laid itself out so clearly. He'd go, making a pretense of fathering, especially in front of his own parents. I'd watch the baby all day, then work for just above minimum wage taking overnight inventory while my parents split diaper duty. The siren calls of nightclubs, beer, and twerking coeds would prove more alluring to Derek than a colicky infant and a residual high school relationship. We'd split, officially. He'd drop out of college, ostensibly to start earning "for the kid", but he'd make me sweat for every dollar of child support. His parents would white-knuckle through babysitting duty while I studied.

Because of one poorly-thought-out night.

"I'm sorry I didn't tell you sooner," I said to Kaitlin.

She nodded, still dazed.

I glanced through the screen door, to the party outside, to Kelsey and Terrence beaming at one another, Makayla inviting Naomi to come visit her during the fall break, Quinn putting on "(I've Had) The Time of My Life". *That's wrong*, I thought. *They've all got beautiful futures lined up right in front of them.* Then I noticed Mrs. Lewandowski through the screen door, cleaning up the sick.

"Jen," I said, "I think I might… waddle home. Can you please just tell your mom it wasn't her coleslaw?"

LINDA MCMULLEN

LUCKY JEFFERSON'S LITERARY ARTISTS

Melissa Eder + Adrienne Green designed the artwork on page 22.

Melissa is an Illustration and Graphic Design student from Germany that loves comics and editorial illustration, that currently resides in Spain.

COUSINS

Mosquitos nibble
our sun burnt skin.
Charcoal smoke
stings our eyes.
We wait our turn for
creamy macaroni salad,
salty potato chips...
Greasy burnt hot dogs
smear ketchup across
our waxy paper plates.
Bellies swell. Time crawls.
Hair sticks to the back of our necks.
Find us rolling
across the fresh cut yard,
vying for spots
under the sprinkler's spray.
Or pressing tushies flat
on the rough sidewalk
leaving damp outlines behind.
Ice cream slips down our arms
as we saunter from
blankets to stoops,
chasing the shade.
The boldest of us
sneaks off
to change the station
from Golden Oldies to Top 100.
Watch us choreograph routines
and style our hair like pop stars,
until we are famished again.
We raid napkin strewn tables
for bakery cookies
and broken up watermelon.

Then plunge our arms
into the cooler's icy depths,
jostling for the last
of the orange soda.
With adults lounging,
kids forgotten,
our tribe of toddlers and teens
spills out of the yard
into the street.
Informal rules, lopsided teams...
Balls land in places they shouldn't.
We don't notice
stubbed toes
or complain about
skinned knees
until the fireflies appear,
the grill is covered,
and our parents load the car to leave.

ERIN MCDONOUGH

DODGEBALL

We scramble to the nest, clutch
a ball, and duck, weave, leap
from the dangers we can see.
There is no tingling inspiration
to snatch us out of the way,

no instinct, no time to dissect
our emotions like we do
for the church or the work
or the government; we have
only the danger and the want.

And when we've been tagged
it's clear to all, and we sit on
the border, sweat down
the minutes left in the game.

JARED PEARCE

MEXICAN SLAYRIDE: MARK 2

B. A. broke through
the swinging doors
and the cartel of Acapulco
came crumbling down
as Murdock with his crop-duster
requested a fly-by.
The title of the episode,
"Mexican Slayride,"
always struck us as odd,
but years later
we understood its full potential.
We invented a drink:
a boilermaker, really.
The Mexican Slayride:
Pour one bottle of Negra Modelo
into a tumbler.
Add one measure of spiced rum.
Repeat…
four or five times
Try it. I dare you!
The perfect beverage
for a summer
evening.

ANDRE PELTIER

SOON

my grandmother always makes me extra rice
when i make my way to her house
crisped at the bottom of a pan and made with love
and secrets i might never be able to understand
i wonder when i might be able to find my way to her house again
its gardens decorated in fake oranges, stone frogs, and pinwheels
merengue snaking its way through the hallways from the backyard
a cold wine cooler from my uncle waiting for me
by her hammock, dusted with still green leaves for good measure
sausages and steaks on the grill
smoke thick enough to make my mother cough
and my uncle laugh

MIRANDA RODRIGUEZ

EVERYBODY HERE

Foil top pulled back & discarded to sip
a barrel shaped drink that turns your
lips & tongue the color of your
favorite fruit: blue raspberry.

Doing the tootsie roll with your cousins
in front of your whole family to a song
you never heard before. *You don't
know nothin' bout this* but your little
brown legs wiggling & twisting all the
same.

Running in & out Auntie's house chasing your
cousin until one of you trip & fall & skin your
knee & mama tells you to *sit down somewhere,
right now* & you imagine the belt stretch out and
curl up tightly around the w in now.

You curl up too - in Auntie's lap, twist the big
gold rings on her middle finger & pick from
her plate of protection & ease-drop on

your oldest cousin's phone call:
Nah girl. Come on. Everybody here.

*Yeah. Mhmm, come round through
the driveway to the back of the house.
And put your dish on the table near
the back door.*

What you bringin?

Good.

*We got all this mac & cheese but
no desserts.*

MAYA LEWIS

LUCKY JEFFERSON'S LITERARY ARTISTS

Joe Bortner + Garrett Zanin designed the artwork on page 30.

Joe Bortner is a comics writer and artist from Massachusetts studying English at the University of Vermont.

WHAT'S NEXT

Upcoming Calls For Submissions:

Issue 8: *Aria*

The curtains are drawn, the house lights dim to dark, a spotlight illuminates the center stage, and an audience anticipates your dramatic verses. This is an open call to all the playwrights (and those new to the craft)! We welcome you to our first collaborative script issue!

To join our production, send us a short unpublished scene that is a continuation of **Act I, Scene I**:

FADE IN:

INT. KITCHEN - AFTER MIDNIGHT

          HIM

    Do you love me?

          HER

    Yes, but when are you leaving?

HIM slams the door so viciously dinner plates backflip off the shelves.
HER collects the cracked ceramic & does not cut her feet on feelings that require therapy.

FADE OUT:

When scripting out your scene, use Scene I as a model and keep these rules in mind:

- Replicate the dramatic structure / format
- Only two characters in the scene: HIM and HER
- Setting can certainly change but keep it realistic
- The scene should not exceed 200 words
- Have fun with stage directions and dialogue
- You are welcome to incorporate poeticness in your scenes

We look forward to watching your verses unfold under the spotlight.

Writing Workshop for *Aria*: Thursday, July 8, 2021 at 6 p.m. E.T. Register at luckyjefferson.com/events.

Early Bird Submissions (free): June 22 – August 22
Last Call Submissions ($2): August 23 – 31
Accepted Playwrights Announced: September 19

FOLLOW US ONLINE

 @lucky_jefferson

 @luckyjeffersonlit

 @_luckyjefferson

USE #COOKOUT, #WHATSCOOKIN, OR #LJSQUAD TO FOLLOW THE CONVERSATION

+

TAKE A SELFIE WITH YOUR COPY OF COOKOUT AND TAG US!